EPILOGUE

Alex,

Have you adapted to your new life? Is your bed made to your satisfaction? Are the sheets soft against your sensitive skin? Do they make your bed with freshly pressed sheets that are tight enough to bounce a quarter off? How has your adjustment been from sleeping on a luxury mattress to a two-inch generic prison mattress on a concrete slab or metal frame, depending on where you are housed? The days feel long, and the nights are short. You have very little privacy, surrounded by strangers from very different backgrounds. Your reality is barbed wire and concrete.

Gone are the days of wearing tailored suits, shirts, and expensive Italian leather shoes. Gone are the days at the beach house, the Murdaugh river house, the Moselle hunting estate, vacations, sporting events, concerts, family gatherings, and flying on private jets.

I often ask myself, at what point did greed, ambition, and lack of empathy overpower you? You had love, family, friendship, respect, and privilege – you had it all, and you decimated everything when you decided nobody deserved to be better off than your family. The lack of values and morals, I believe you had at one time, was overcome by the grandiose and extravagant lifestyle that people close to you had achieved. I now see you for what you are. You always needed to be around people different from you so you could watch as they marveled and bragged about being friends with Alex Murdaugh.

For many years, I witnessed your interactions with people and your ability to make them feel special and important, regardless of their background. You easily blended with people from all walks of life. Not very many people can say or do that, but you did. You were such a dedicated father and husband, always making time for your family.

Your gregarious personality was one of the qualities I admired the most about you. You appeared to be honest and open. It was also one of the reasons why I didn't give it a second thought about working with Maggie. I feel betrayed. I never imagined that my decision to help Maggie would have such a significant impact on my life. Your wife was a fantastic woman who loved you, pampered you, and took pride in your accomplishments.

She didn't understand your taste for sweets, but she always made sure you had plenty, from the Froot Loops to the chocolate milk to the Capri-Suns. She felt that your child-like eating was cute. Spoiling you became her priority, especially when the boys were away in school.

I still remember walking into the house one morning after Maggie and you went to a movie. She laughed when she said she didn't care too much about the movie, but your gesture made her feel special. She sounded like a high school girl who had gone on her first date and couldn't wait to tell someone about it. She acted the same way when you gave her the much-publicized Gucci purse, when you took her out to dinner, or when you went away on the weekend to the mountains.

What happened to you? What happened to the man who was always entertaining by cracking jokes; what happened to the man who nurtured and cared for his family? At what point did you become so unhappy in your life that you decided to kill your wife and son?

You were born into a family with money, power, and privilege—a legal dynasty established by the Murdaugh men who came before you. You were already enjoying the fruits of your ancestors' labor, but you wanted and felt the need for more and more. You possessed the qualities necessary to be a political success, potentially serving as governor of the state at some point.

Your entitlement and greed destroyed lives. Being the son of Randolph Murdaugh III and the grandson of the great Buster Murdaugh, you felt entitled. The life you once knew will never be the same. Maggie and Paul are only memories from your past. Why weren't you honest with Maggie about your financial problems and let Paul face his consequences? You could have saved his soul, eased his pain, and been the father that he craved. Instead, you valued your legacy over his life. I can still see Paul climbing into bed with you, sharing his day, or lying there, happy to be near his dad. Do you remember those days? I do.

Your actions that night were those of a coward who failed to face the reality of his own actions.. I questioned your behavior during and after the funerals, observing your gestures and facial expressions. I noticed how people approached you, something they would never have done if Maggie were alive. I especially remember an unfamiliar woman wandering around the house as if she owned the place, almost as if announcing to the world, "This will be mine."

I believe you confessed to the murders of Maggie and Paul to your dying father, Mr. Randolph, whispering words like, "Daddy, I messed up bad, really bad, Daddy. Tell me what to do." But we will never know.

Maybe, as Judge Newman said at your sentencing, you might have been someone else that night due to your opioid use. What were you thinking when you decided to pull the trigger?

As you sit alone in your assigned cell, hopefully, you are taking the time —because time is what you have plenty of —to review the decisions you made and stop believing the lies you told. I hope you are asking God for forgiveness every day and every night. Your choice to destroy your family to gain sympathy overshadows the love and protection you owed them as a father and husband. I may never find the answers that bring me full closure, but for now, I am releasing the emotional burden of your betrayal and focusing on my own healing.

Praying for you,
Blanca

Finding Blanca

My journey into the Murdaugh family saga began with the shocking murders of Maggie and Paul Murdaugh in June 2021. As the high-profile trial unfolded, one figure stood out: Blanca Turrubiate-Simpson, the family's loyal housekeeper, whose testimony from the witness stand gripped the courtroom. Her words carried weight, revealing intimate details about the Murdaugh household that went beyond the prosecution's questions, offering glimpses into a world few outsiders understood. Blanca's proximity to the family gave her a unique perspective, one that resonated deeply with those following the case.

About a year after the trial, I felt compelled to explore the broader impact of Alex Murdaugh's actions—his financial fraud, addiction, and the murders that shattered lives. My goal was to connect with victims, both those directly harmed and those caught in the emotional fallout, to understand how one man's betrayal rippled through a community. I reached out to family members, friends, and others whose lives were upended by Alex's crimes, hoping they'd share their stories. Most declined, their reluctance understandable; they wanted to leave the pain behind and avoid being defined as victims. I respected their choice but pressed on, determined to uncover the human toll of the Murdaugh saga.

When I contacted Blanca Turrubiate-Simpson, I braced for rejection, expecting her to guard her privacy as others had. To my surprise, she was open to talking. After a lengthy phone call, she agreed to meet my collaborator, Dr. Michelle DuPre, and me in Walterboro, South Carolina, the heart of Murdaugh country. It was a blistering July day, with temperatures soaring to 98 degrees, but the heat couldn't dampen our anticipation. Over hours of conversation, Blanca shared stories of her time with the Murdaughs, including her bond with Bubba, the family dog she adopted after the tragedy. Bubba played a pivotal role in the trial; his presence at the kennels contradicted Alex's alibi and contributed to securing his conviction. Blanca's affection for Bubba was deep, a testament to her deep connection to the family she served.

One moment from our time together stands out vividly. Blanca and Bubba took me to the graves of Maggie and Paul. When we arrived, Bubba leapt from the truck, sniffed the air, and found their headstones. Without hesitation, he lay down between them, curling up as if to keep watch over them. It was a heartbreaking yet profound scene—Bubba seemed to carry the weight of that night, missing Maggie and Paul as deeply as any human. That moment underscored Blanca's role, not as a housekeeper, but as a keeper of the family's untold stories.

Despite the flood of books, documentaries, podcasts, and news coverage about the Murdaugh case, Blanca's perspective has been largely overlooked. Many dismissed her as a peripheral figure, assuming a housekeeper had little insight into the family's inner workings. They were wrong. Blanca was more than an employee; she was a confidante, particularly to Maggie, privy to the private joys and tensions of the Murdaugh household. She heard lies in court—distortions about the family she cared for and even about herself—and faced rumors that twisted the truth. Maggie's mother, Kennedy, trusted Blanca with a mission: to ensure the real Maggie, not the media's version, was remembered. Blanca felt a duty to set the record straight, to honor the family she loved while confronting the painful reality of Alex's betrayal.

At first, Blanca hesitated to share her story publicly, wary of being misrepresented or exploited by the media frenzy surrounding the case. She waited for someone she could trust, someone who listened without judgment and amplified her voice authentically. Through our conversations, I earned that trust, a responsibility I don't take lightly. Together, we embarked on a journey to tell her story, one that captures not only the Murdaughs' downfall but also Blanca's resilience and compassion. Our collaboration has blossomed into a deep friendship, forged through shared purpose and mutual respect. Blanca is a remarkable woman—strong, thoughtful, and unwavering in her commitment to truth.

   With deep appreciation,
   Fran

ACKNOWLEDGMENTS

Blanca Turrubiate-Simpson

The love of God, family, and friends has been my strength while writing this book. I especially want to thank my husband, Michael, for encouraging me when I didn't believe in myself. His suggestion to write down what I was feeling and his encouragement to tell my story are what have helped me get this far. He was the voice of reason, peace, and calmness amidst the emotional rollercoaster I was on. I love you, Michael.

Michael knew the Murdaughs and interacted with Maggie and Alex throughout the years. He knew Maggie well through their personal conversations or her animated, silly phone calls after football games. Maggie was always boasting about her fantasy boyfriend, Tom Brady, to get a rise from him.

To this day, I can still hear her voice saying, "Tell Michael to go suck a lemon," over a football game, and remember Maggie's kind gesture of preparing meals not only for her family but also for ours.

Michael said, "Those memories of Maggie are what people need to know about, and only you can share those stories." But the question to myself became, how am I going to do this? How do I find a coauthor? People who had approached me wanted my story for themselves and for me to step back. Then, I met Fran Weaver. We clicked immediately, and the writing began. It has truly been a team effort. Our circle expanded with the creation of Chick-a-Dees Media (Maggie's nickname for me), led by Cassidy Pierce. Thank you so much for your love and support.

I want to thank my children for being patient with me when I didn't cook for them during their visits. That must have been disappointing. I will make it up to you soon!

To Ms. Kennedy Branstetter (Maggie's mother), I still remember standing next to you at the entrance to the dining room at Moselle as you held my hand for support and told me not to turn any opportunity away from telling my story about Maggie. Thank you for your blessings, for the trust, love, and support you continue to give me to this day.

Kudos to the extraordinary, strong women who stepped up to make this book a reality: my coauthor Fran Weaver, Michelle DuPre, Valerie Bauerlein, Kristina

Greene, and Cassidy Pierce. I want to thank Emily D. Baker and her many fans of the Law Nerds for your supportive comments. To Molly C., you listened with no judgment and understood my pain while guiding me through the trauma throughout the chaos. Enjoy your retirement.

My sincerest gratitude to my sisters in Christ from the Macedonia Women's Ministry for consistently reminding me to lean on my faith in God for strength during difficult times.

To my dear friend, Angie Hickerson, the best neighbor anyone could have. Thank you for continuously allowing me to express my feelings and lean on you when I felt down and depressed. You give me strength and encouragement. Thank you, and continue to be the amazing, strong woman that you are.

A very special thank you to Don Weaver, who put up with me as a guest in his home while Fran and I worked on the book. You are the best! I also want to add my thanks to Dr. Welker and his staff for checking on me and ensuring I was okay.

Finally, I extend my sincere gratitude to Ms. Barbara Mixon, as well as to all the housekeepers who work tirelessly every day. Your efforts transform homes into clean, welcoming spaces; your skill and commitment create comfort and order for countless families. Thank you for your resilience, professionalism, and the pride you take in your work—you make a difference every day.

My world is brighter because of all of you. Thank you from the bottom of my heart.

ACKNOWLEDGMENTS

Fran Weaver

If someone had told me I would become an author in 2025, I would have laughed hysterically. *Writing Within the House of Murdaugh*...and forming a close friendship with Blanca Turrubiate-Simpson has been truly inspiring, driven by passion, perseverance, and a strong sense of teamwork. This is Blanca's remarkable story. I was lucky to be part of her journey. It was Dr. Michelle DuPre, a nationally known forensic pathologist, who challenged us to keep going when we questioned our path and were honestly scared to reveal certain pieces of her story.

This book was made possible by the collaboration and expertise of many exceptional individuals. First and foremost, my husband Don, who initially thought I was delusional when I started this journey. However, when he saw that the book was real, the saying "seeing is believing" comes to mind. He has become my source of strength. Thank you, my love.

I want to thank my amazing family who have kept me on the right track for telling Blanca's story - Katie Hoffecker and Shellie Beasley, my ever-supportive, encouraging, and brutally honest, twin daughters; Denice Kennedy, my step-daughter who I am proud to have in my life and has stood by me step-by-step in this process giving her honest feedback; and Kristina Greene, an honorary member of our family who has volunteered her guidance since day one.

Most especially, Cassidy Pierce, who is doing an incredible job directing our social media and publicity campaigns and happens to be my granddaughter. My pride and love for her are so profound that I can hardly contain myself. She continues to amaze me every day with her intelligence, strength, and resolve. We certainly could not have done this without you!

Darby, who watched me struggle and offered validation; my ever-encouraging Madison, whose marketing ideas were spot on; and Eli, who has grown into a young man so quickly. Please know that I pull my strength from you - watching your success in your endeavors. You make my heart full.

I extend my deepest gratitude to my circle of strong, supportive women who assisted me in this process. From the beginning, my high school classmate, Lee Ann Sigmon-Farley, encouraged me repeatedly to persevere and not give up, even when I was close to the edge. That circle of friends extends so wide that I honestly cannot express my gratitude enough.

Kim Bolser, my incredible friend and colleague for many years; Emily Acuff, my steadfast friend who has always been there for me when I needed her the most; Muriel Crawford, the most incredible woman I have ever met who has supported me through all of my trials and tribulations; Pamela Marsh, my longtime friend who introduced me to Don and assisted with the initial editing of the book; Barbara Gibson, my forever friend and head cheerleader; Maxine Beckner, my social media BFF; and Barbara Christmas Golden, my treasured mentor and beloved friend who instilled many of my Southern traits.

Sincere thanks are extended to Joe McCulloch, an outstanding and notable attorney in Columbia, South Carolina, who followed every aspect of the Murdaugh saga. He sealed our partnership by providing advice and protecting us from sharks who sought to gain control of this book.

I sincerely thank everyone who contributed to this collaboration. This one's for you!

About the Author

 Blanca Turrubiate-Simpson was born in Brownsville, Texas, in 1967. After high school graduation, at the age of seventeen, she left her hometown to join the US Navy. The highlight of her career was steering a ship across the Atlantic Ocean. After leaving the Navy, Blanca became a correctional officer at Ridgeland Correctional Institution in Ridgeland, SC, and later transitioned to employment with the Federal Bureau of Prisons in Estill, SC. Her bilingual skills secured her a job as a Special Investigation Support Technician in the Special Investigative Office. Her skill at profiling Hispanic gang activity within the prison earned her a spot in an investigative training school in Colorado, which led to swift promotions.

Blanca met Alex Murdaugh while assisting a Hispanic friend with a legal matter at the law firm of Peters, Murdaugh, Parker, Eltzroth, and Detrick (PMPED) in Hampton County, SC. On an as-needed basis, Blanca assisted Alex as a translator.

Soon after, Blanca began working for Maggie Mudaugh, Alex's wife, as a housekeeper and personal assistant. For more than a decade, Blanca worked for the Murdaughs, earning Maggie's trust, respect, and friendship. After suffering a stroke in 2015, Blanca took a leave of absence to receive medical attention and rehabilitation. Shortly after Paul's boat accident, she resumed her responsibilities with the Murdaugh family.

Since the murders of Maggie and Paul, Blanca has become a recluse, rarely venturing far from home. She and her family adopted Bubba, the beloved dog of Maggie and Paul, who played a critical role in Alex Murdaugh being found guilty of their murders. After four years of much thought and prayer, she chose to write a book that humanizes and honors Maggie and Paul.

About the Co-Author

 Mary Frances "Fran" Weaver grew up in Morganton, North Carolina, and attended Greensboro College in Greensboro, North Carolina, as well as the University of South Carolina in Columbia, where she earned her undergraduate degree in education and her graduate degree in rehabilitative counseling. She has served as a crime victim advocate and a lobbyist for educators in both South Carolina and Georgia. Fran was the lobbyist who successfully led the movement in Georgia for legislation to reward educators, both monetarily and professionally, for achieving National Board Certification.

Fran was a specialist in curriculum software, serving as the Southeast Regional Director for a national curriculum company headquartered in Chicago, and for Curriculum Advantage, which launched the national award-winning *Classworks* software. Most recently, Fran served as a Channel Partner for Centegix's *CrisisAlert*, the award winning proactive crisis management platform for school safety. Now retired, she concentrates on her writing.

Her fascination with high-profile criminal cases at the state and national levels drew her into the true crime phenomenon. Living in South Carolina and loving the Lowcountry, she was especially interested in the crimes of Alex Murdaugh in Hampton County, South Carolina, as she had known some of the players in the saga.

Fran lives with her husband on Lake Murray in Chapin, South Carolina, and enjoys spending time with her adult children and their families. She enjoys traveling, entertaining, spending time in Hilton Head, and indulging in her favorite pastime—writing.

APPENDIX

The Murdaugh Family

Randolph "Buster" Murdaugh Sr. (1887–1940)

- Patriarch and founder of the Murdaugh legacy
- Graduate of the University of South Carolina School of Law, 1910
- First Murdaugh elected solicitor of the Fourteenth Judicial Circuit in South Carolina
- Solicitor 1920–1940
- 1940, killed when struck by a train
- Prepared his son, Randolph, Jr., to become a solicitor

Randolph "Buster" Murdaugh Jr. (1915–1998)

- Graduate of the University of South Carolina School of Law, 1938
- Solicitor 1940–1986
- Known for his courtroom antics

Randolph "Mr. Randolph" Murdaugh III, "Handsome" (1939–2021)

- Graduate of the University of South Carolina School of Law, 1964
- Succeeded his father as solicitor in 1986
- Solicitor 1986–2005
- Returned to his law firm, PMPED, until his retirement
- Died June 10, 2021, three days after the murders of his grandson, Paul Murdaugh, and his daughter-in-law, Maggie Murdaugh

Randolph III and his wife, Elizabeth, "Libby," had three sons and one daughter:

Lynn Murdaugh Goettee (1963 -)

- Eldest child and only daughter of Randolph III and Libby
- Alex's older sister
- Graduate of Columbia College, Columbia, S.C., 1985
- Victim advocate for the First District Solicitor's Office, Charleston, S.C.

Randolph "Randy" Murdaugh IV (1966 -)

- Graduate of the University of South Carolina School of Law, 1991
- Partner at The Proctor Group law firm (formerly PMPED), Hampton, S.C.
- Alex's older brother

John Marvin Murdaugh (1970 -)

- Graduate of the University of South Carolina, Criminal Justice
- Businessman owns farm equipment stores in Hampton and Okatie, S.C.
- Alex's younger brother

Richard Alexander "Alex" Murdaugh Sr. (1968 -)

- Graduate of the University of South Carolina School of Law, 1994
- Former Partner at PMPED law firm, Hampton, S.C.
- Found guilty of murdering his wife, Maggie, and son, Paul, on June 7, 2021
- Found guilty of numerous financial crimes, including stealing from clients and his law firm
- Incarcerated for life at an unknown South Carolina correctional facility

Margaret "Maggie" Branstetter Murdaugh (1968–2021)

- Graduate of the University of South Carolina, 1990

- Married Alex Murdaugh, 1993
- Two sons, Richard Alexander "Buster" Murdaugh, Jr., and Paul Terry Murdaugh
- Died on June 7, 2021, at Moselle in Islandton, S.C.
- Alex Murdaugh, her husband, was found guilty of her murder

Richard Alexander "Buster" Murdaugh Jr. (1996 -)
- Graduate of Wofford College, 2018
- Married Brooklyn White, May 2025
- Alex and Maggie's older son

Paul Terry Murdaugh (1999–2021)
- Junior at the University of South Carolina, majoring in Criminal Justice, at the time of his death
- Father, Alex Murdaugh, found guilty of his murder committed June 7, 2021
- Alex and Maggie's younger son
- Died on June 7, 2021, at Moselle in Islandton, S.C.
- Alex Murdaugh, his father, was found guilty of his murder

(DuPre, M., 2023. *Money, Mischief, and Murder.* Chapter 2. pp 19–25.)

(DeWitt, M., Jr., (2024) *The Fall of the House of Murdaugh.*)

Reference List

We wish to acknowledge the reading and referencing of the books listed below, indicating that the work influenced our thinking, even if specific details aren't directly cited in the text.

Bauerlein, Valerie. (2024). *The Devil at His Elbow, Alex Murdaugh and the Fall of a Southern Dynasty.* (1st ed.). Ballentine Books.

Berry, J. R.(May 18, 2023). *Meet Bubba, the family dog that helped convict Alex Murdaugh of double murder. WLTX19News.wltx.com.* https://www.wltx.com/article/news/special-reports/alex-murdaugh/bubba-the-dog-alex-murdaugh-trial/101-0c469de4-1bba-4053-b920-f2a43de8c456.

Cawthon, G. (2023, March 3). *Murdaugh Timeline of Evidence: This is what happened the night Paul and Maggie were murdered.* WJCL 22 abc. Retrieved September 5, 2024, from https://www.wjcl.com/article/murdaugh-murders-timeline-evidence/42846491. (The timeline, in italics, used throughout Chapter Twelve, is taken directly from Cawthon.)

Chappell, B., and Hansen, V. (2023, March 3). *Here are 8 big revelations from the Alex Murdaugh murder trial.* www.npr.org. Retrieved September 6, 2024, from www.npr.org/2023/03/01/1160319398/alex-murdaugh-murder-trial-revelations.

Crime & Cask, (2023). *Defending Alex Murdaugh – Not Guilty by Reasonable Doubt* (1st ed.) Amazon Publishing.

Dewitt, M., Jr. (March, 2023). *Alex Murdaugh trial: What we know about Paul's 2019 boat crash.* Information retrieved from: https://www.greenvilleonline.com/story/news/local/2023/02/02/alex-murdaugh-trial-what-we-know-about-pauls-2019-boat-crash/69867668007/. *Greenville Online.*

DeWitt, M., Jr., (2024) *The Fall of the House of Murdaugh. Moonshine, Manipulation, and Murder in South Carolina.* (1st ed.). Evening Post Books, Charleston, SC.

DuPre, M. (2023). *Money, Mischief, and Murder* (1st ed.). Self-Published.

Elassar, Alaa & Vogt, Adrienne, *Here's What the Judge that Sentenced Alex Murdaugh Said,* (March 3, 2023), CNN US – Crime + Justice. Retrieved August 16, 2024.)

Glatt, J. (2023). *Tangled Vines - Power, Privilege, and the Murdaugh Family Murders* (1st ed.). St. Martin's Publishing Group.

Murdaugh Murders: A Southern Scandal. Documentary series. (2023). Netflix. Episode 3: *The Roadside Shooting* (Director: J. Meek)

Oppenheimer, Jess. 1951-1957. *I Love Lucy.* Hollywood: Desilu Productions.

Ryan, J. (2024). *Swamp Kings* (1st ed.). First Pegasus Books.

Rossignol, Rosalyn (2018). *My Ghost Has a Name: Memoir of a Murder* (1st ed.) University of South Carolina Press.

CREDITS

Palmetto Publishing,
Charleston, S.C.
Front and Back Cover Design

Cassidy Pierce,
Director of Social Media and Publicity
ChickaDeesMedia.com
Photography, Audio, Video
Columbia, S.C.

Rebekah Hickerson Photography
Lexington, S.C.
Front and back cover photos